Old BANFF & MACDL

by
Alan Cooper

Lipton, Low Street, 1937. It is believed that Lipton's first shop in Banff was in Carmelite Street.

ISBN 1 84033 085 6

FURTHER READING

The books listed below were used by the author during his research. None of them are available from Stenlake Publishing. Those interested in finding out more are advised to contact their local bookshop or reference library.

The Ogilvies of Banff, C. Abercromby, 1939.
Life on the Low Shore, P. Anson, 1969.
The Annals of Banff, W. Cramond, Vol. 1, 1891; Vol. 2, 1893.
The Making of a Banffshire Burgh, W. Cramond, 1893.
Duff House, I. Gow & T. Clifford, 1995.
A History of Banff, J. Imlach, 1868.
The Building of Duff House, J. Simpson, 1973.
Banff in Old Picture Postcards, I. Strachan & B. Carter, 1995.
Lord Fife and his Factor, A. & H. Tayler, 1925.
Macduff and its Harbour, 1783-1983, anon.

ACKNOWLEDGEMENT

The publishers would like to thank Robert Grieves for providing the picture that appears on page 47.

The publishers regret that they cannot supply copies of any pictures featured in this book.

The Turrets was a quaint old house in the High Street that was demolished to make way for the new museum and library, opened in 1902. Fred Cooper described it as 'a beautiful old building' (*Banffshire Journal Annual* 1977, p87) and recalled how as a boy he had watched the stonemasons shaping the stones for the new building.

INTRODUCTION

When A. A. Cormack made an enquiry in 1960 to the town clerk of Banff, he was astounded to learn that all the early documents and records of the royal burgh had been disposed of during the First World War as waste paper. Fortunately for Banff, William Cramond, the historian of Banffshire, published two volumes of extracts from the records in 1891 and 1893 under the title *The Annals of Banff*. These provide a wonderful insight into the social and economic conditions that prevailed in Banff from the seventeenth century onwards.

The seventeenth century in Scotland was a lawless and violent age, and some of the worst offenders were members of the nobility. Sometimes minor disputes turned very nasty. In 1628 in the tolbooth of Banff, Lord Banff struck his relative James Ogilvie of Auchiries on the head with a baton during a court case. Twenty of his friends and followers then attacked the man with their swords, before chasing him into the street where they finished him off by shooting him with a pistol.

Despite widespread lawlessness, ordinary people were subjected to rigorous discipline and rather severe regulations. In 1743 James Cant of Achluncart and his wife and two daughters were imprisoned in the tolbooth for allegedly setting fire to some corn stacks – they were later transported to the West Indies. Peter Young and his wife were imprisoned for breaking into a house at Portsoy in 1787. Young escaped from the tolbooth but was recaptured and tried in Aberdeen where he was sentenced to be hanged. After another escape, he was hanged in Edinburgh in 1788. In an age when sexual activity outside marriage was an offence, one case in Banff in 1661 was remarkable: 'Thomas Stewart, Laird of Bog, had fallen in fornication for the fyfth time, and this time in the tolbooth with a woman put in ther for murthering a chlyd. . . . The ministers of Fordyce and Deskford are to be sent to speak with him' (Cramond, vol. 2, p37).

Servants were often subjected to restrictions, for example in 1682 it was decreed that: 'no man's servant nor woman servant be fund out of thair maisteris hous efter nyn hours at night' (Cramond, p161). In 1728 'all brewers are discharged from alloweing servants, apprentices, and jurneymen from playing at cairds and dyce under penalty of £6 Scots, whereof a third shall go to the informers' (Cramond, p199). Many activities were banned, for example in 1682 'players of football on the streets to be fined 40 shillings' (Cramond, p161). In 1702 'an act against pipers and promiscuous dancing was read and approven' (Cramond, vol. 2, p73). In 1706, 'there is ane vicked custome in this place used by several idle persons in mascarading and profane gulling with antique faces, men in women's habits and antique habits afrighting the inhabitants, women and children' (Cramond, p177).

The lowest class was made up of beggars and vagabonds, who were perceived to pose a threat to law and order and were treated with the utmost severity. In 1703 'it was recommended to the Magistrates to take up lists of loose and vicious persons who haunted this place, that they might be expelled hence' (Cramond, vol. 2, p74). During the same year 'the Dean of Gild and Conveener, members of the Session, were appointed to take up lists of all the poor idle children within the town that they might be disposed on . . . to apply some lawful calling'. And later in 1703 'The Magistrates did undertake to dispose of them so as to prevent any disorders or abuses by them, especially on the Lord's Day' (Cramond, vol. 2, p74).

People who had committed a relatively minor offence were sometimes seized by their neighbours, tied by the hands and feet to a thick pole, and then paraded through the streets in what was called 'riding the stang'. In 1740 six men were fined for taking Mrs Ann Smith from her house and 'mounting her on a tree and carrying her through the streets, and considering the midwife's report as to the state of her health . . . ordain them to be imprisoned in the tolbooth . . . until it be found she is out of danger' (Cramond, p153).

The eighteenth and early nineteenth centuries saw great progress in transport and communications in Banff, with the first Deveron Bridge completed in 1765. A public meeting was held in 1800 at which a resolution was passed 'to make a Turnpike Road between Turriff and Banff, the existing road being then almost impassable' (Cramond, p350). The establishment of two branch railway lines, the Macduff to Turriff Railway (1860), and the Banff, Portsoy and Strathisla Railway (1859), provided a connection with the main Aberdeen to Inverness railway line, and an impetus for the development of trade. Macduff, with its increasingly well-developed harbour facilities, prospered in a modest way, along with the adjoining settlement of Banff.

The first Deveron Bridge opened in August 1765 but was swept away by a flood on 16 September 1768. The present bridge, designed by John Smeaton, was finished on 17 June 1780 and replaced a ferry-boat then in use. Prior to the building of the bridge the King's Foord, situated where the Gelly Burn joined the Deveron (about half a mile south of the bridge), was used to cross the river. The original road connecting Banff town with the ford on the river passed very close beside Duff House. In 1756 the Duff family made arrangements with the town council to divert the road away from the house and along the side of the river instead, although permission to do this had apparently been obtained some years earlier: '1735, June 7. William Duff of Bracco gives in compliment for the use of the harbour of Guthrie ten gunneas in gold, the community having readdily agreed to his altering the road which leads from the King's Foord to the town' (Cramond, vol. 2, p223).

Salmon fishing was once an important industry on the Deveron at Banff, employing many people in netting the fish, salting them, packing them in barrels and shipping them. There is a reference to salmon in 1250 and again in the oldest existing burgh charter (1372), when the fishings were granted to its inhabitants. In 1471 the town rented out the fishings to Sir James Ogilvie of Deskford and others. Under a charter granted by James VI in 1581 the magistrates were given the power to rent out the salmon fishings in perpetuity, but only to merchants or inhabitants of the town. In the 1620s and 30s the fishings brought in £54 yearly, about 20% of the burgh's annual income. By purchases in 1692 and again in 1705, Alexander Duff of Braco came into possession of almost all the fishings, even though according to the charter of 1581 he could not purchase them. He eventually passed them on to his nephew William Duff, first Earl Fife. In a dispute over unpaid tax in 1710, magistrates seized four barrels of fish belonging to Duff.

THE RACK, NEAR BANFF.

In 1769 the council decided to let the fishings in the sea to the west of the mouth of the river. Lord Fife took the town to court, however, obtaining a judgement that 'the said Earl has right to, and been in possession of the whole salmon fishings in the sea, and opposite to the river or water of Doveran' (Cramond, vol. 2, p258). Despite this the magistrates continued to let the disputed fishings, which were eventually purchased by the 5th Earl Fife for £4,205 in 1863. Fife's ownership of fishing rights near the mouth of the Deveron had a significant effect on fish stocks upriver: 'Lord Fife's cruives, which are only a short distance above the mouth, intercept the majority of the ascending fish, the upper proprietors get a very insignificant share of salmon until the nets are removed. After that the angling is better.' (Cramond, vol. 2, p261, quoting from a book by Holdsworth & Young, 1877.)

In May 1735 William Adam was engaged by William Duff of Braco to build Duff House, and construction started soon afterwards. There appears to have been no contract, nor any estimates given as to the cost, however, and the men fell out and became involved in a dispute. This was not settled until April 1746 when £2,576 was awarded by a court to Adam against his outstanding bill for £5,720. The long wings in Adam's original plans were never built, by 1746 the house was still unfurnished, and William Duff never lived in it. Duff became Baron Braco in July 1735, and then Viscount Macduff and Earl Fife in 1759. Though he and his descendants are often referred to as Earls of Fife, the title was 'Earl Fife' until the 6th Earl married the Princess Royal, daughter of Edward VII. He was created Earl of Fife and then Duke of Fife. When Robert Southey, the Poet Laureate, visited Banff in 1819 he described Duff House as 'a square, odd, and not unhandsome pile' (Cramond, p254).

Entrance to Duff House Grounds, Banff

As the MP for Banffshire, James Duff, second Earl Fife, spent most of his time in London, but his thoughts often returned to Duff House and he wrote constantly to his factor, giving him detailed instructions, as in this letter dated 30 December 1768: 'You are to be particularly attentive to everything about the house, the farm and the policys, see that nobody be allowed to walk thro' the garden, to see all doors and windows of the house locked every night, every person about the house regularly go to bed, that the iron gate always be locked, except when Lady Fife orders it not, the peats and coal cared for, the horses cared for and see they be put to work, the servants both at the farm and barns well employed, the smith and smiddy looked after, the cows cared for, and the dairy keept right, that no person be allowed to hunt or any way disturb the game, to prohibite foot walkers, horses and carriages from going thro' the barns to the foord, and that the gate at the barns be locked every night, the corn under the charge of the grieve, the cattle feeding under his charge keept well sight of and everything else clear accounts to be kept of.' (Tayler, p50).

The Bridge and Hill o' Doune Banff.

In 1746 a doctor with Cumberland's army wrote that Banff had 'two small harbours for shipping but large vessels cannot come near them' (Cramond, p128). Of these two harbours one eventually became Banff Harbour. Situated at the mouth of the River Deveron, the other was a natural harbour that owed its existence to a bank of sand and shingle called the Bar which used to extend across the bay. This bank was moved by the tides, closing the mouth of the river at times. There are references in the town's records to ships being pulled over the Bar, and in 1689 the magistrates requested that 'at least furth of everie family be sent for helping to haill in the ships' (Cramond, vol. 2, p214). In 1890, when the shallowness of the water prevented salmon from entering the river, 20 men worked to cut a channel through the bar, but their efforts were repeatedly undone by the sea.

The building in the centre of the picture was the grammar school from 1780 until 1838 and the office of the *Banffshire Journal* from 1845 to 1982. Originally a single storey building, it was heightened by six feet in 1796 using stones from the old church nearby, but in 1805 was taken down and rebuilt as the two-storey building that is still in use today. In 1780 the headmaster was Alexander Johnston, who earned £20 a year plus 40 percent of the fees. Subjects taught were Latin, Greek, writing and figures (arithmetic), plus bookkeeping and navigation in the evenings.

When applying for the post of headmaster, Alexander Johnston wrote 'Whatever follies while a young man I may have been guilty of, these are now over, and even my enemies will allow me never to have neglected giving due attendance at school hours; it must therefore be apparent, since my engaging in the family way with so agreeable a young woman as to have fallen to my lot, that I will rather encrease than diminish my diligence that I may always maintain her in some degree becoming a Magistrate's daughter' (Cramond, vol. 2, p90). Two years later Johnston was dismissed 'having given no regular attendance for many months past, by which the school is totally lost. The second master has gone to be master of the Grammar School of Elgin' (Cramond, vol. 2, p190). In 1836 the school building was declared to be 'unwholesome and subject to frequent inundation' (Cramond, vol. 2, p198) and the pupils were transferred to new buildings in 1838. The sender of this postcard has written: 'This is Banff on Thursday. We had a terrible thunderstorm the whole day.' The date of the storm was 19 June 1913.

Sir George Ogilvy, first Lord Banff, had a palace between what is now Carmelite Street and Bridge Street. Along with its enclosed orchard, this was completely destroyed by the army of General Munro in 1640, as described by Patrick Gordon of Rothiemay: 'In the verie heart of the towne stood Banfe's pallace, high built and quarterlie, the structure magnificent. . . . Upoun it the soldiours fell and in a few days defaced it leaving nothing to be seen but defaced walls' (Abercromby, p50). In compensation for his loss, Ogilvy was granted 19,000 merks by Charles I, and raised in the peerage to a baron under the title Lord Banff. A Carmelite monastery existed in or near Banff until the Reformation, but its exact location is a matter of dispute. William Cramond, the historian, firmly believed that it had stood outside the town. He concluded that the ruins near Carmelite Street, claimed by many to have been monks' cells, were the remains of Lord Banff's palace, although he admitted that he was unable to persuade anybody to agree with him!

Rose's Temperance Hotel was built on the site of the old prison usually called the tolbooth, which was in ruins by the 1790s and was sold by the council at a public auction in 1801 or 1802 to William Reid, town clerk, for £56. It had been built in 1712 and replaced an earlier tolbooth on the same site. It was a large two-storey building with prisoners confined to the upper floor, access to which was by a stone stair on the Strait Path. Prisoners could converse with people on the street through iron bars, and small gifts could be passed through to them. In 1739 Ann Mowat was banished from the town for passing through an iron bar, and in 1712 some prisoners almost escaped by setting the door on fire. James Macpherson, the freebooter, was held and sentenced to death at the tolbooth along with James Gordon. The execution (by hanging at the Cross) took place on 16 November 1700, the men having been found guilty of 'in ane bangstrie manner, going up and doune the country armed, and keeping mercats in ane hostile manner' (Cramond, p101).

Left: The erection of the Market Cross can be dated to the period 1627-1628 when items of expenditure in the town's accounts relate to the 'new croce'. This was situated where the Biggar Fountain was later built, and mounted on a huge hexagonal base, about fifty feet in circumference, with a door on the outside. In 1748 a man was ordered to stand with his back to the door for two hours with a sign reading 'an infamous outhounder of thieves', to 'outhound' meaning to incite to mischief or crime (Cramond, p316). In 1768 the town council applied to the court of session for permission to move the cross: 'It is herein stated that the Cross is a pretty large building, inconvenient for town and country people resorting to the annual or weekly fairs, these being held in the street where the Cross now stands' (Cramond, p315). Soon afterwards it was moved and re-erected by Lord Fife on a hill at the end of Sandyhill Road. The base (the Doocot) remains there today, though the actual cross was moved to Low Street in 1900.

Right: In 1762 the council decided that a steeple should be erected to hold the town bells and a clock, and the foundations for this were laid in 1764. In an age when very few had clocks and watches were rare, it was important that people knew the time so that they could attend church services and knew what time to go to work and retire to bed. In 1714 a bell was rung at 5 a.m. and again at 9 p.m. with a drummer and piper sent out at 4 a.m. and 8 p.m. to reach those further away. There were complaints that the men were failing in their duties in 1720. This was possibly due to the weather, as the council had given instruction that on rainy nights William Anton should beat his drum in the tolbooth with the doors and windows open, rather than actually walking the streets! A new court house and prison were built next to the steeple in the years 1797 to 1800 at a total cost of £935, replacing the tolbooth which had become ruinous. The Biggar Fountain was erected in 1878 in memory of Walter Biggar, an Edinburgh man who settled in Banff in 1821 and 'became the founder of the Continental herring trade' (Cramond, p377).

LOW STREET BANFF.

From 1638 to 1770 there are many references in the town's records to the problem of middens in the streets, and in 1770 there were complaints about middens at the entry to the churchyard. Pigs were banned from the town in 1653 because they were destroying corn and kale, but the ban must have been unsuccessful as it was reiterated in 1666 when geese were also prohibited. Pigs were banned again in 1702 unless they were kept indoors – anybody who found a pig doing damage in a garden was allowed to kill it. During the same year twenty-five people were fined one merk each for allowing cows, horses, ducks, geese or pigs to graze on other people's ground.

BRIDGE STREET, BANFF.

Within a few years of the Deveron Bridge being opened in 1765, walls and gates were erected around the grounds of Duff House, preventing direct access from the bridge to the main streets of the town. Carmelite Street became the main route into Banff, and in 1768 to ease the flow of traffic the Market Cross was moved from the end of Low Street. At the time Carmelite Street was a lane, only ten or eleven feet wide in places, and the following year the council opened a new street, which they named Bridge Street. When the bridge collapsed in 1768 the King's Foord was used to cross the river again. The council applied to the Government for money towards rebuilding the bridge, although they were concerned that poor access to the town might hinder or prevent their application from being granted. It was probably after the opening of Bridge Street that the markets were moved to Market Place (renamed Old Market Place after 1831).

For many years after the battle of Culloden soldiers were stationed in Banff. A guardhouse and sentry boxes were built for them, as well as a military hospital in the Seatown (1757). In the same year a new guardhouse was built at the top of Bridge Street, on the north side. One young soldier to do garrison duty there was James Wolfe, who went on to command troops at the capture of Quebec. A letter from him written in Banff dated 1751 has survived. In 1771 William Robinson, a thread manufacturer in the town, became involved in a dispute with some officers who had been drinking in the Black Bull Hotel. Returning to his house in Low Street, he found the soldiers in a courtyard with some of his nursery maids. A scuffle followed, but ended soon afterwards when one soldier fetched his sword and ran it through Robinson. Two lieutenants, Gibbons and Thorn, were imprisoned from 22 April until 26 May accused of murder, but were released when the King's Advocate refused to prosecute them.

LOW STREET, BANFF.

Gammie. Photo.

William Robinson's house at 15 Low Street, visible on the extreme left of this picture, has the date 1745 above the middle window. The garrison in Banff provided husbands for many local women. Cramond records that 'in 1751 six Banff women married soldiers in the regiment of Foot commanded by Hon. Lieut. General Pulteney. In September and October 1755, there were six similar marriages with the soldiers then stationed at Banff, and in 1761, when the Scots Lowlanders and 71st Regiment were at Banff, were other six' (Cramond, vol. 2, pp290-291).

The poet Byron was born in London on 22 January 1788. His mother, Catherine Gordon, inherited the estate of Gight and the farm of Monkshill at Fyvie, as well as salmon fishings on the river Dee, but these were all sold to pay off her husband's debts (Gight was sold to Lord Haddo for £17,850). Mrs Byron and her son lived in Aberdeen from 1790 to 1798 and for a spell in 1795 with her mother in Banff at her house in Low Street (pictured left). The house was demolished to make way for the new Sheriff Court and County Buildings, which were opened in January 1871. There is a tradition that the young Byron robbed a pear tree in the minister's garden, and Cramond mentions that he was referred to as 'that little deevil Geordie Byron'. He also mentions an incident when Byron butted a Miss Abercromby of Birkenbog 'like a ram and threatened to throw her over the balcony. Byron had then arrived at the mature age of seven or eight years!' (Cramond, p236).

Right: In 1779 the second Earl Fife agreed to give ground at Little Fillacap for the building of a new church; in return he requested the Gaws and a small piece of land below the bridge. He also offered to make a road along the south side of the proposed church at his own expense, if the town council would close off the public road to the Old Lodging (which stood within his lands) and give him that road in return. Soon afterwards the Earl's factor at Duff House wrote that 'the Colly Road is now shut up, and all communication with the town of Banff blocked up, except from the gate at the bridge, and where the new gate is to be' (Cramond, p328). The new church of St Mary was built between 1789 and 1790, and a steeple was added in 1849. A large bell was placed in the steeple in 1851, following which the town managers decided that the town drummer should stop his march round the streets and ring the bell every morning at 5.45 a.m. instead. Rev. Bremner refused to allow this, however, as the permission of the minister, heritors and kirk session had not been obtained. The town managers countered by pointing out that the bell had been placed there by public subscription, and threatened to remove it. It is not recorded whether this resolved the dispute.

Collie Road joined the southern ends of High Street and Low Street, and another connecting road led to the King's Foord until the Fife family moved the road to the edge of the river to prevent the public from walking across their land. There were a number of complaints about this, particularly as the Duffs only came to Duff House for a month or two in the summer and for a spell at the end of the year, spending most of their time in London. In a letter dated 8 September 1763, William Rose, the factor, wrote: 'The Magistrates of Banff is saying that your lordship is obliged to erect a bulwark from the end of the old one all along to the King's Foord. A late high tide has been the cause of moving them to this, for it came as far as to make it impossible to go dry-footed betwixt the bridge and the town' (Tayler, p13). Lord Fife wrote to his factor on 30 March 1765 that 'There is nothing I want so much as a Park keeper . . . nothing makes the place so disagreeable as the crowd of idle people that are walking over my grounds' (Tayler, pp15-16). Collie Lodge was a gatehouse to Duff House.

In 1838 the grammar school moved into new premises at Wilson's Educational Institution, which also housed a museum and library. The institution was built with money from a legacy left to the magistrates of Banff by James Wilson, a Banff man who had died at Grenada. In 1846 the rector was paid £80 a year, and his two assistants received £15 a year plus the fees from their own classes. There were 758 children in the burgh between the ages of five and thirteen in 1873, and 671 of these were attending one of the seventeen different local schools. Girls were allowed to join the classes at Banff Academy for the first time in 1866, and in that year Saturday morning classes were discontinued and replaced by a full day on Wednesday instead of a half day.

SANDYHILL ROAD BANFF.

In 1823 the population of Banff was concentrated in the two main streets in the lower part of the town, and the Seatown. Sandyhill Road did exist, but Wilson's Educational Institution had not yet been built on the glebe and further along there were just four residences at the end of Gardiner's Brae, two on either side. In his *History of Banff*, published in 1868, James Imlach stated that the last portion of land to be acquired by the Duff family from the town council was 'the beautiful lot of land stretching along from the Church of Banff southwards to the Sandyhills, sloping down from the road' (Imlach, p11).

Writing about his youth in Banff in the early 1900s, Fred Cooper remembered that Sundays were very solemn days, and that 'to ride a cycle or even to run was a deadly sin' (*Banffshire Journal Annual*, 1974, p129). In the town's church records there are many references to sabbath-breaking. Activities that landed people in trouble included killing a sheep (1666), gathering seaweed (1676), drying clothes (1692), striking a boy (1693), carrying burdens (1695), 'vaging' (walking or wandering) (1705), and brewing a kettle (1722). Offenders were usually given a warning, though some were fined and ordered to appear before the congregation. An article in the burgh records related to proper conduct on a Sunday: 'June 19, 1709. The minister advertised the people of the town (particularly servants) to keep within doors on the Sabbath and to read or hear what may be edifying and may tend to the good of their souls and not vague in the streets or about the seaside, as has been represented they too often do.' (Cramond, vol. 2, p78).

In 1732, as punishment for a minor offence, James Wood was ordered to clean the High Street from the Grey Stone to the Episcopal Chapel and 'to carrie off the muck, stones or other rubbish' (Cramond, p205). The stone stood opposite the top of the Strait Path, and marked a spot where people gathered to discuss the news and gossip of the day. John Wesley preached there in May 1776. The Grey Stone was last mentioned in the records in 1834 and according to Cramond disappeared afterwards when the ground was levelled. There was a cistern for water near the stone, and another one near the Market Cross. In 1763 it is recorded that 'As the present two cisterns for the town are far too small, and the water often deficient . . . the Town Council resolve to remove the present cistern at the Cross and place it where the other is, viz. at the head of the Strait Path, and to have a new and larger one at the Cross' (Cramond, p310). However, in 1777 it was reported that 'The cisterns of the town's wells being in disorder, a plumber is to be sent for from Aberdeen or elsewhere' (Cramond, p326).

Government forces led by the Duke of Cumberland arrived in Banff on 10 April 1746 in pursuit of Prince Charles Edward Stuart and his rebel army. On their way they destroyed all the Episcopal chapels they could find, and at Banff broke the organ, burned the pulpit, altar, seats and books and tore down the roof. A man who was thought to be making notches on a stick (and thereby counting the strength of the army) was seized and immediately hanged as a spy. Lord Braco, afterwards first Earl Fife, had met Cumberland in Aberdeen, anxious to display his loyalty and protect his valuable estates from being plundered. Several of his family were with the rebels including his son-in-law, Sir William Gordon of Park, and two brothers-in-law. His eldest son, a drunken and dissipated young man of whom little is known, also wished to join the rebels but was restrained on the orders of his father. One of the nine people from Banff listed as being involved in the rebellion was George Abernethy, a merchant and magistrate in Banff and a captain in the rebel army.

The sender of this postcard has marked with crosses Mr Mudie's church, his manse, and then 'the hall where the classes are held'. In May 1843 Rev. Francis W. Grant was minister at St Mary's, the Established Church in Banff, a post he had held since 1821. As a result of the Disruption, he resigned and joined the Free Church, taking about half his congregation with him. To begin with they worshipped in the Congregational Church in the Seatown, but the foundation stone for their own church was laid in August 1843, and it opened about May 1844. Pictured above, it was designed by Mr Raeburn of Edinburgh, architect, cost £1,800, and had seating for about 800. The manse was built in 1845 at a cost of £500. In 1914 the Banff Free Church congregation united with that of the United Presbyterian Church, and in 1994 reunited with St Mary's, from which it had split in 1843.

Seafield Street was opened in 1852 and replaced Boyndie Street as the main road into Banff from the west (St Catherine Street was the main road into the Seatown). At the end of the nineteenth century, Seafield Street was still known locally as the New Road, and was a favourite place with both young and old for sledding in the winter months. The church on the right of the picture has had a very unusual history. Built in 1880, it served as the United Presbyterian Church until 1914 when it became redundant due to the merger with the United Free Church. In 1926 it was bought by the Whitehills United Free congregation, dismantled stone by stone, and transported three miles to Whitehills and rebuilt there. A clock was added to the tower, gifted by the Misses Addison in memory of their parents.

The bowling club was opened in Seafield Street in 1903 and replaced a bowling green in Boyndie Street, behind the present Town and Country Club. The postcard was sent in August 1904 and bears the message: 'I am sure a sight of all these worthies will be as good as a visit to Banff. You will know lots of them'. A new pavilion was opened in the summer of 1981.

Prior to the building of Seafield Street, the main road from Portsoy came through Boyndie Street. There were houses along Boyndie Street and also Gallow Hill Street, but the area between these streets and Sandyhill Road was undeveloped. It was the same on the other side of Boyndie Street, with fields as far as St Catherine Street. The Seatown, reached by Castle Street, was part of Banff but had its own distinct identity. It comprised a number of streets above and below Castle Street including Fife Street and Back Street (Clunie Street). There was a brewery, lime works, and the harbour nearby. A battery had been built in 1781 when the council felt the threat of invasion was likely. Embrasures were constructed and mounted with two cannons to fire 18 pound balls and four to fire 12 pound balls, but in 1815 the battery was dismantled and the coastguard station was built there later on.

CHALMERS HOSPITAL & CLUNIE ST. BANFF. N° 3

In 1757 a soldiers' hospital was built in the Seatown; it was apparently only ever used by the military, and closed after the garrison had left the town. In the valuation of lands and property belonging to the burgh in 1835 the old hospital was valued at £10, and in 1858 it was reported as having been sold. The town council were always reluctant to provide a hospital for the local population, apparently on grounds of expense; on at least two occasions money earmarked for a hospital was used for other purposes. In 1789 George Smith of Bombay died at sea and left £1,000 in his will for building a hospital, but the money was used to build the new Town House and prison instead. By providing a soup kitchen in the Town House for the poor in times of need, the council felt that it would be satisfying the terms of the bequest. A similar diversion of cash occurred in 1841 when the council decided that £200 raised for the building of a hospital several years previously should be used for other purposes within the town. Alexander Chalmers bequeathed his estate for the building of a hospital, and the foundation stone for this important facility was finally laid on 10 July 1861.

Banff was the headquarters of the Banff, Portsoy and Strathisla Railway, many directors of which were local landowners or businessmen. The company was established in 1857 with the aim of opening up a new line from Grange to Portsoy and Banff, and the line was opened on 2 August 1859 with intermediate stations at Knock, Cornhill, Tillynaught and Ladysbridge, with a branch to Portsoy from Tillynaught. Trains ran to a temporary terminus at Banff Links until the Harbour Station was opened to traffic. The passenger platform at the Links (above), officially known as the Golf Club House Halt, was opened in 1914. Banff Links Golf Club was established in 1871 with fourteen members, and remained in existence until 1923 when it amalgamated with Duff House Royal Golf Club. Fred Cooper recalled that golfers were expected to wear a bright red jacket and cap, and when teeing off would shout 'fore' as a warning. His father made his own gutta-percha balls by pouring the molten rubber into a mould. Clubs used at that time were a driver, brassie, lofter, cleek and putter (*Banffshire Journal Annual*, 1974).

It is likely that golf has been played in Banff for hundreds of years, as in 1637 it is mentioned in the town's records that Francis Broune was hanged for the theft of items including some golf balls. Broune's trial was held in the tolbooth on 9 September 1637 where he had been held securely in the stocks following his arrest on the 6th. He had broken into a booth in the market place during the night and stolen many items including coins, plaiding (woollen cloth), a pair of gloves, a brush, a comb, as well as 'sume golff ballis' (Cramond, p78). The items were recovered and Broune confessed to the crime and admitted that he had sold two of the golf balls to Thomas Urquhart, a servant. The court took the opportunity to convict Broune for various other crimes, including stealing corn from the fields at harvest time, failing to attend church services and being a 'leud liver and boy of ane evill lyiff' (Cramond, pp78-79). The sentence of the court was 'to be presentlie tackin and cariet to the Gallowehill of this burghe and hangit on the gallows thereof to the deathe' (Cramond, p79).

Alexander Dawson started working for the Banff, Portsoy and Strathisla Railway as a supervisor at the crossing near Mill of Boyndie soon after the railway opened in 1859, and was still working there when this photograph was taken in 1905. He lived in the cottage nearby and also worked as a tailor – there were only three or four trains each day and probably not much in the way of road traffic at that time. Dawson had a son who was a stationmaster; two of his grandsons were stationmasters, and two of his granddaughters were married to stationmasters. In November 1901 a tramp/labourer was killed at the crossing when he was hit by a train. The gatekeeper hadn't seen him and had signalled to the driver to proceed. The man, of unknown identity, was aged about 70, and had called earlier at Mill of Boyndie where he had been supplied with food (*Banffshire Herald*, 9 November 1901). The last passenger train on the line left Banff in July 1964.

Ladysbridge Asylum was built by Banffshire Lunacy Board and opened in May 1865 with accommodation for ninety patients and boarding charges of £23 10/- per year. Previously the nearest asylum for the insane had been in Aberdeen. There is a reference in the burgh's records to a case in 1837 when a patient was sent to Aberdeen on the advice of his doctor, but after spending £7 on his boarding charges, the Kirk Session decided that they could not continue to support him. Three months later the hospital threatened to remove the patient and the Session sent a further £12, but resolved to recover as much of the money as possible by asking for subscriptions. When in 1759 Fordyce Kirk Session had a problem with somebody who was insane they decided that the only thing they could do was order the making of a wheelbarrow so that the woman could be transported around the parish in the hope of receiving charity from the parishioners.

SCOTSTOWN BANFF.

In 1759 John Leall, fisherman, was engaged by the council and received money for building a house in the Seatown, as well as for a line and an oar (*sic*). The following year the council paid £5 for a new boat, and fixed the rents to be paid by the fishermen in the Seatown (eight names were listed, including one woman). By 1809 fish had to be brought from Whitehills and Macduff as Banff's fishermen were reduced to four old men, although four men from Buckie, comprising a boat's crew, were persuaded to settle in Banff with the offer of a boat and houses which were to be rent-free for seven years. Several other crews settled there soon afterwards. In 1853 seven fishermen from Portknockie were engaged and £300 provided for building six houses for them along the seashore. The settlement became known as Scotstown after William Scott, Provost of Banff from 1844-1850 and 1851-1853.

The Banff, Portsoy and Strathisla Railway's Harbour Station (above) was opened to traffic (though not passengers) on 31 March 1860, when a goods train with eleven wagons and a carriage with some of the directors arrived at 4 o'clock to be met by crowds of spectators on the braes, along the shore and at the station. 'The engine bore in front a masonic flag and was smartly busked with evergreens' (*Banffshire Journal*, 3 April 1860). At Tillynaught Junction the line divided into two, with one part going along the coast and the other inland via Cornhill to join up with the main Aberdeen to Inverness line. The income generated covered the railway's running costs, but not the interest on bank loans, and in 1863 the GNSR agreed to work the line in return for 60% of the company's receipts. It amalgamated with the GNSR in 1867 when the line was renamed as the Banffshire Railway. The last passenger train ran from the Harbour Station left on 6 July 1964.

Banff Harbour was originally called Guthrie's Haven, and the first reference to it dates from 1625 when James McKen of Fraserburgh was engaged to dig out rocks from the small creek. The building of the harbour proceeded very slowly, with progress hampered by a chronic shortage of cash. Often work that had been done in the summer was destroyed by winter storms. By 1698 there was one pier, but the harbour was often filled with shingle and sand, rendering it useless. In 1726 it was reported that several recently-loaded ships had to be unloaded again, as there was not enough draught in the harbour for them to sail from it. The Commissioners appointed by the Convention of Burghs visited Banff in 1726 and reported that: 'Guthrie's Haven is extremely well situate . . . has a good foundation for building a pier, water is deep, and access is easy, even with northerly winds, which is a great advantage, considering that from Aberdeen to Inverness there is not a harbour that any ship dare adventure to seek into, when the wind blows in from that airt' (Cramond, vol. 2, p221). By 1744 there must have been several piers as quarry-men were engaged to dig out rocks 'beginning at the side of the little middle pier' (Cramond, vol. 2, p228). Construction continued and it was reported in 1760 by a Bishop Pococke that there were two piers suitable for taking ships of 100 tons. Between 1770 and 1775 a new harbour was built at a cost of £4,000, to designs by John Smeaton. The piers of the old harbour were taken down at the same time. Major works costing £14,000 were undertaken in 1818-1819, based on the plans of Thomas Telford, though 'the opinion of local fishermen and sailors afterwards prevailed with Telford to modify his plan so as to extend the outer quay 150 feet till it covered the mouth of the old harbour' (Cramond, vol. 2, p236).

"ON THE LOOKOUT," ®

The view overlooking Banff Harbour, with Macduff in the distance. In 1746 a doctor with Cumberland's army wrote of Banff that 'the town, I believe, lives chiefly by smuggling' (Cramond, p128). Certainly the importation of goods including tea and brandy without paying duties was very common at the time. It took place in all classes of society, and even Earl Fife preferred to smuggle things, at one time writing to his factor about wine he was bringing in from Rotterdam, saying that it 'must be keeped secret as Baillie Hay [in Banff] would be very pleased if our cargo was seased' (Tayler, p23). The lack of a customs house in Banff was a great hindrance to trade in the eighteenth century. Permits had to be obtained from Aberdeen before ships could be loaded or unloaded, and a trip on horseback might take several days, during which perishable goods could be ruined. The small depth at many of the creeks and piers at Banff Harbour meant that when ships were loaded they could sometimes only get out and in upon spring tides.

In 1754 it is recorded that 'The Council grant ground to Bailie Philip to build warehouses near the harbour at a feu-duty of ten shillings' (Cramond, vol. 2, p228). There was a great scarcity of food in 1766, to the extent that people were starving and some desperate locals boarded a ship and stole some food. The case is mentioned in a letter dated 20 June 1766 from the magistrates in Aberdeen to the magistrates in Banff: 'No doubt you have heard of the riotous mobb that happened here on Friday last at the whipping of the three criminals in pursuance of the sentence of the Circuit Court in May last for the riot they were guilty of near Banff, by assisting to rob a ship of meal. The three prisoners were rescued by the mobb, and we can get no account of which way they went' (Cramond, p313).

The fire at Stevenson & Asher's boat-building yard on 6 May 1912 started in or near the engine-house just before 10 p.m. and spread very quickly, sending flames and sparks shooting up into the sky and attracting hundreds of spectators. The long wooden building had recently been tarred and was highly inflammable. The fire brigade arrived quickly and though they could not save the building did prevent the fire from spreading to a sawmill and to the two boats on the slip of the yard. One of these, the steam drifter *Gleam of Hope*, was only a few feet away and became so hot that hissing steam could be seen rising from her timbers, although continuous hosing with water prevented her from burning. By 11 o'clock the boatyard had been reduced to smouldering ruins and the spectators had gone home. Luckily the evening had been very calm, otherwise wind could have spread the fire much further.

The Macduff to Turriff Railway was opened on 4 June 1860 with intermediate stations at Plaidy and King Edward. It was an extension of the Turriff to Inveramsay line, opened on 5 September 1857 with stations at Auchterless, Fyvie, Rothienorman and Wartle. At Inveramsay Junction, four miles north-west of Inverurie, the line joined the Aberdeen to Inverness main line. On 1 July 1872 Macduff Station (above) and Banff Bridge Station, situated half a mile apart, were opened to replace the original terminus which had been called Banff & Macduff Station. This had been inconvenient for both towns and was demolished the same year that the new stations opened. The Macduff to Turriff line officially closed to passengers on 1 October 1951 and was closed completely on 1 August 1961. Macduff Parish Church was built in 1805 and enlarged in 1865 when the original steeple was removed. At the same time the church became part of a *quoad sacra* parish with a permanent minister.

Though Banff and Macduff lie in the same bay and are only a mile apart, the River Deveron separates them. Before the opening of the bridge in 1765 people could walk across the river at the King's Foord or take the ferryboat. In one incident in 1739 the ferry was carried out to sea and at least four people drowned, the only survivor being a Mrs Shand from Doun (Macduff) who happened to be carrying a large sack of wool on her back which kept her afloat until a boat arrived. The incident is mentioned briefly in the minutes of the town council: 'By the careless conduct of Alexander Steinson, present tacksman of the ferry boat, their happened yesterday a very melancholy accident, by his trusting the ferry boat to a boy who by his want of strength and skill, occasioned the loss of severall people's lives' (Cramond, p212). A letter from Sir William Dunbar to Lord Fife in 1773 mentions another accident: 'We propose to have a ball for relieving widows and bairns of the boatmen and people in Down, drowned on Friday morning last . . . the seven lives lost call loudly for a bridge' (Cramond, p320).

The burgh of Macduff was originally part of an estate called Glendowachie, which included the small town of Doun or Down. In 1733 the property was bought by William Duff, afterwards Earl Fife, and it was his son, the second Earl Fife, who started the rapid development of the town and its harbour, especially after 1783 when he obtained a new charter for the burgh and changed its name to Macduff. He effectively named it after himself, as Viscount Macduff was his title when his father was still alive. The first Provost of Macduff, 1783-1798, was the Earl's factor, William Rose, who was heavily involved in the town's early development. The relationship between the men ended in acrimony, however, with Rose suing the earl and taking his case to the House of Lords. He had been paid £100 a year as factor but felt that he had done a lot of other work, both legal and political, for which he had not been paid. Nonetheless he lost his case, plus a legacy of £500 which the earl cancelled. He nearly became bankrupt and was so bitter that he wrote in his will in 1803 that 'It may happen that the man called Lord Fife may oppress my wife' (Tayler, p271).

The second Earl Fife regularly wrote to William Rose regarding Macduff. In 1783 he stated that: 'I flatter myself to see the place thrive under your auspices, numbers increasing, trade and manufactures flourishing' (Tayler, p149). During the same year he wrote to say 'I would have you call a few friends and christen Down. . . . I can afterwards have another day for founding the new pier and Macduff's Cross which I intend to build'. A communication of 1786 instructed Rose to 'settle with the Down fishers and prosecute those who are not paid up' (Tayler, p51), while in 1789 he said: 'I wish much that more people would settle in Macduff. I think shipbuilding should be promoted' (Tayler, p197).

In 1759 Down (Macduff) had 34 tenants, and the community of about 400 lived mainly by crofting. The town had five boats and two yawls at the time, and fishing was probably used only to feed the community, rather than generate revenue. Each boat had a crew of six men and each yawl two men. By 1783 there were 134 tenants and the population had increased to over 1,000. There were 7 boats, 30 to 40 yawls and 5 large vessels of 10 tons which were employed in carrying fish to the Firth of Forth, bringing goods to Macduff and, in the summer, fishing for skate, haddock, cod and ling. In 1714 Banff Town Council allowed two men to work at Down harbour, carrying away the rocks that quarry-men were digging out. However, the development of the harbour really began under Earl Fife and his factor, William Rose, and a new harbour was completed soon after the town's name was changed to Macduff. The harbour has been developed and expanded several times since.

The Fishers Return.

601

Line fisherman William Lyall with his grandchildren at Rob Laing's pier, Macduff. This ancient pier, a small jetty, disappeared when the Princess Royal Basin was constructed during the years 1914 to 1920, 'the engine house and the slip-way being later built on top of it' (*Macduff and its Harbour, 1783-1983*, p59). The picture was taken by Macduff photographer J. Ritchie, Jun.

Morrison Brothers garage in Skene Street, with the iron railings of the garden to Manor House, a shell-covered house built by Dr Walford Bodie, just below it. Bodie was a famous theatre and music hall entertainer who married Jeannie Henry, a girl from Macduff. She appeared in his show as Princess Rubie; her sister was called Mystic Marie; and another relative went under the name of La Belle Electra. The latter was once put into a box and buried six feet underground for twenty minutes at Macduff. During the stage show La Belle Electra could apparently make herself light or heavy, and resist the efforts of six men to lift her. Bodie was born in Aberdeen in 1869 and his real name was Samuel Murphy Brodie. He and Jeannie had three children, Jeannie, Albert and Sam. There is a memorial fountain to Jeannie in Duff Street. Bodie made a huge amount of money from his shows but he was extravagant, and Manor House and its contents were sold off in the 1930s to pay debts, along with a luxury houseboat on the Thames and a theatrical club in London.

Manor House, Skene Street. Walford Bodie's performances included magic, stage hypnotism, electrical effects, ventriloquism, healing of incurables and bloodless surgery. He was a master of showmanship and usually started his shows with a demonstration of his electrical powers by passing 30,000 volts through his body (although unknown to his audience he used static electricity, which produced a lot of sparks but was harmless). At one time he used an electric chair, but would switch off the power when the subject started to turn a black colour! In 1920 his friend Harry Houdini gave him the actual chair used in the first execution of this kind in the USA in 1890. Bodie's use of hypnotism and electricity to cure 'incurables' was dependent on having a number of assistants planted in his audiences. His use of the doctor's title MD was unpopular, especially with medical students in Glasgow who pelted him with missiles in 1909 and deliberately stopped his show. Famously he always maintained that MD stood for Merry Devil! Bodie died in 1939 and was buried in Macduff.